MAKE

Volume One

Our Maker Life, for makers by makers

The Heart of a Maker

It is our heartbeats that I truly believe guide the journey of *Our Maker Life*. What started from a prayer placed on my heart has culminated to the lovely beats of your stories, patterns and pictures that prove what I have always known deep down inside: the maker life is beautiful.

My maker life began from something rather un-beautiful – anxiety, depression and a fearfulness to search and uncover the pages of my spirit with boldness. But then I picked up my first set of needles and yarn. And right there, in casting on 40 stitches, I found courage and learned something about myself: I have the power to live pretty brave. I discovered that courage is beautifully enthralling and quite possibly the core of a maker's heart. As is peace, appreciation for slow living, laughter, imag-ination and a deep determined love to make life work – to trust the journey – and to believe that even if we do not know why a story began a certain way or exactly how it will end, we can read in between the lines and find something more beautiful than we ever really imagined.

Because our stories are enchanting and what make us our bravest. Our brave heartbeats are why my OML team and I produced this book. Through the Our Maker Life movement, we have reached thousands and thousands online. However, we also believe there is a classic beauty to print. A beautiful reminder that while we can admire it, we are not to judge each other like one may judge a book by its cover – because we are much more than that.

Here in between the first vol-ume pages of *MAKE* we aim to bring you maker stories, patterns and look books that portray a true and traditional beauty of the maker life. Here are our goals and dreams come true. Our hopes for more. Our beauty from ashes. And we hope that you will take the opportunity to sip a warm beverage, turn a page, smile, and know that you too possess the tools to live pretty brave.

Because your heartbeat is perhaps the strongest and most courageous craft tool you have.

So smile. Soar. Take a chance. Be brave. Embrace life, love, and make.

It could be the most beautiful journey you ever take. xo

- Jewell Washington
Our Maker Life, Founder
Northknits, Shop Owner

CONTENTS

STORIES

Big Dreams Start Small

By Macy Sheaman
I'm Crazy for Craftin'

I'm crazy for crafting. Always have been.

When I was little, and the house grew quiet, my mom always knew exactly where to find me: elbow-deep in glitter and glue, creating my next masterpiece.

I'm 15 now, and my crafting has evolved beyond glitter and glue, but I experimented with a lot of different crafts before I settled on making knitwear.

When I was seven, my grandmothers taught me to knit and crochet, and I've loved making yarn creations ever since. But at seven years old, I wanted to try every craft that interested me. My local librarians knew me by name and were always on the lookout for good craft books to satisfy my current whims. I made candles, soap, paper, clay beads, and jewelry; it wasn't long before I was running out of space to store all of my creations!

So, at 10 years old, I decided to solve that problem by starting a crafting business.

My family supported and encouraged me every step of the way. I designed and printed my own business cards and began selling my wares at church bazaars, yard sales, and to family and friends.

By June 2014, when I was 13, I was ready to open my own Etsy Shop, *I'm Crazy for Craftin'*.

I mainly feature yarn crafts in my shop, but I also sell sewn and repurposed accessories. It makes me so happy to know my items are being enjoyed by people all

over the world.

Besides making crafts, I enjoy other aspects of running a business, like photographing my designs for new products. I also like researching the latest fashion trends and experimenting with new yarns, stitches, and techniques. When I first opened my shop, I wanted to sell a wide variety of items, but I quickly learned that it was better to make a few things and make them well. I scaled back on my jewelry-making, so I could devote more time to my first love: yarn crafts.

My mind is constantly brimming with ideas for new designs. Planning and dreaming are some of my favorite aspects of the creative process. Sometimes I get so excited about a new idea I can barely go to sleep at night!

People often ask me how I have time to run a business and keep up with my studies. I'm blessed to be homeschooled which allows me to start on my schoolwork early in the day and then work on what I really love. Running a business counts as schoolwork too as I've learned so much about business, marketing, advertising, photography, mathematics, writing, and more.

And in case you're wondering, yes, I do have a social life. I've learned to balance my schedule between family, church, school, business, and friends.

The holiday season is busy with craft shows and fulfilling orders, but one of the things I love about knitting and crocheting is that it's portable. I can take my yarn and needles almost everywhere, and I do. I make scarves and hats at my brothers' ballgames, at youth group, while watching TV and listening to music, and while riding in the car.

"Don't you ever get tired of making all that stuff?" People ask.

No. I really don't. I'm blessed to love what I do. And even now – when the house grows quiet – my mom still knows exactly where to find me.

Darling, Be Brave

By Megan Aldred
Darling Be Brave

When I was a child, if someone told me that someday I would run my own business, one that required me to constantly put myself out there for the world to see, I'd have nervously laughed in their face and not believed a single word.

I've always been a tender hearted wallflower, a little shy and way too introverted, the kind of person who would rather blend in than be the center of attention. I did all the normal things you're supposed to do: graduate high school, college, get a degree, but I always felt kind of lost. And when it came time to conquer the world and find a career, I didn't know what to do. I couldn't think of a job that I would be happy dedicating 40 hours a week to for the rest of my life.

During my last year of college, at 22, freshly married and itching for a hobby, I purchased a set of crochet hooks on a whim. I had grown up with a grandmother who always had a hook or needle in hand, and I found the craft so fascinating. I remember watching her in amazement, noticing the fluidity of her hands as she worked the yarn and needles, making something so beautiful out of such simple tools.

It thrilled me to discover that learning to crochet came naturally. I became an addict, spending all my spare money on yarn, making project after project. I just couldn't put it down. I've since fallen in love with knitting as well. It's more of a challenge, but I enjoy it just the same.

About a year later, I stumbled across Etsy's website for the first time. In an instant, a whole world of possibilities opened up to me. An entire community dedicated to selling handmade goods? I could hardly believe it! I felt a fire and passion I had never felt before. I so desperately wanted to be a part of this community, convinced that if those people could sell their handmade creations online, I could too.

Soon after, I opened up a little Etsy shop and started posting pictures to Instagram of my work. Little did I know that this would completely change my life.

I started gaining followers and making some truly amazing friends. I found out that crocheting isn't just a little old lady hobby. There's an entire community filled with the most kindhearted and talented people. I had finally found a place where I belong, where I fit in.

But I, perhaps, jumped a little too quickly into Etsy though. Without much thought, I picked the shop name One Loop at a Time (which I'll admit I still love), but after a while I felt stunted, almost as if I had hit a wall. I wasn't exactly sure where I was heading, but I knew deep down that One Loop at a Time wasn't going to get me there. I needed a name that inspired me.

At that time, it seemed everywhere I turned, the phrase, "be brave" kept popping up. Call me crazy, but I felt like it was the sign I was looking for, an answer to my prayers. I had been living life

10

> *"I had been living life as a timid wallflower, and it was time for me to be brave."*

as a timid wallflower, and it was time for me to be brave. Time for me to fully live my life the way that I wanted to instead of always doing what was expected of me. Time for me to be brave enough to accept myself just as I am with all my weird quirks and traits. And most of all, it was time for me to be brave enough to be myself even though I've always felt like who I am is so different than everyone around me. I was ready to whole heartedly jump into this, turning my shop from a hobby to an actual business.

Through all these thoughts, Darling Be Brave was born. This name is a sweet and gentle reminder to do the things I love each day without fear of judgment, to pursue my passions and dreams without inhibition.

Darling Be Brave is the prompting I need to be fearless and to push myself to do the things that I've always wanted to do. Darling Be Brave helps me to embrace and be more open with who I really am as an individual. It helps me to get out of my shy shell. I love

having my shop name be my own personal mantra. And more than anything I hope that whenever someone sees Darling Be Brave, it encourages them to be a little more brave too.

Never in my wildest dreams would I have thought that I could find a career that included playing with yarn every day, taking beautiful pictures and making friends along the way. It's almost unreal to look back and see how far I've come.

It's such a wonderful feeling to know that people around the world know who this shy little wallflower is and that they enjoy my creations. I have been unbelievably blessed in my journey, and I'm so grateful to be where I'm at today.

My story may not be the craziest or the most exciting, but hopefully it's one

that many can relate to. It's proof that anyone, even the quiet awkward girl from high school, can do anything they set their mind to. All you have to do is be brave and take a chance.

Living the Simple Life

By Hailey Smedley
Ozetta Handmade Knitwear

My story begins at a young age when I would stay with my great-grandmother Marjorie Ozetta, who taught me the foundations of knitting and crocheting. I would stay with her for weeks in the summer months, and we would wake up early to cook breakfast (she made the best homemade cinnamon rolls), watch movies, and curl up in her handmade quilts, crocheting. She always said, "Little Hailey, you can do anything."

I remember the first thing she taught me to make was a forest green blanket for my dolls. It may have taken me just short of a year to complete (with the edges being not so straight) - but I was proud of what I had created.

Even at that age, I fell in love with the idea of taking a skein of yarn and making it into something tangible. After that, I would pick up my needles every year around the holidays, but when my grandmother passed away in 2007, I picked them up and never put them down.

I wanted to keep her memory alive in some way, so Ozetta Handmade Knitwear began. She left a legacy behind that still remains the core of who I am and what my shop is based upon. If I could impact others, and do so in her name, then I consider this the strongest foundation of what I love doing. I think when people read about my shop, they feel as though they are wearing a part of a story, and to me this is more important than anything. After all, there is truly nothing greater than the coziness of handmade knitwear.

I love the connection of knitwear and nature. I draw most of my inspiration from those fall mountain roads, needle tree lined hills, and rainy days. The organic feeling of being inspired by something, and watching it grow by making it with your own hands is nothing short of magical.

My shop has given me the chance to be my best person and has ignited something sustainable to work and live for. When you are surrounded by something you love doing, you become greater. When you invest your creativity and hard work, it shows.

I have found in the most recent years, that being creative is not just a business opportunity, it is a chance to make connections with those that share in the same dream as yours.

Additionally, Ozetta has given me the chance to stay at home with my two little ones and enjoy time with them while they are young. My hope is that one day they will feel the impact my great grandmother had on me, and in turn fill their lives with what they love doing.

I live a very simple life filled to the brim with cozy days and lots of coffee, surrounded by my family in a place I love. I wouldn't trade these days for anything.

"I love the connection of knitwear and nature. I draw most of my inspiration from those fall mountain roads, needle tree lined hills, and rainy days."
- Hailey Smedley, Ozetta

Finding Purpose in our Unique Talents

By Toni Lipsey
TL Yarn Crafts

The birth of TL Yarn Crafts came from my desire to be a worthy steward of this amazing life I am blessed with. I have always believed our existence is a divine circumstance and it should not be wasted. I spent a long time trying to figure out the purpose of my unique mix of talents, and the process of finding a worthwhile preoccupation was a long one. Shortly after finishing graduate school and getting married, I found myself in an emotional rut. I was un-

inspired with no clear sense of what the next steps were for me. I had completed my education, found a loving partner, and created a home for myself. But something very important was missing. After months of this funky mood, it just clicked. And for the first time in my life, I felt the longing to make.

My first foray into craft as an adult was friendship bracelets. Because who doesn't love friendship bracelets?! Two weeks and a lot of wasted embroidery floss later, I was over it. I returned to the craft supply store shortly thereafter with an open mind, ready to be inspired. I strolled through aisles of glitter pens, and silk flowers and eventually found myself stopping in the yarn aisle. The nostalgia immediately enveloped my like a warm hug. My yarny instincts kicked in and I started squishing the yarn, remembering how the different weights and fibers felt between my fingers. Though at the time I did not know where this adventure would take me, I finally felt like I was moving in the right direction.

The vivid memory of how I learned to crochet replays in my mind constantly. It was a sweltering mid-summer day in suburban Detroit. I was 13 years old and bored out of my mind. It was the kind of bored that makes every possible remedy seem absurd. And it was annoying my mother (though she would likely deny it). After I meandered into the room where she was sitting for about the fifth time that afternoon, she finally set down her own knitting and started fiddling with some purple cam-ouflage yarn. I glanced at it disinterestedly and started walking out of the room. I hear my mother say "Here" and I quickly returned to her side. A couple minutes later, I was on my way to making a granny square blanket. Mom told me to keep going until I ran out of yarn, then she gave me more. When I was finished, I had what was likely the most dreadful blanket ever made. But it was mine, it was done, and I had made it with my own two hands. This victory is squarely in my Top 5 memories, falling just behind marrying my best friend and holding my newborn niece. I have no idea where my first granny square blanket is now, but I like to think it is folded at the foot of someone's bed, ready and waiting.

My mother, Gwendolyn Jones, is by far my greatest inspiration in life and in craft. Not only did she teach me to crochet and knit, but in that she taught me patience, perseverance, and trained me to explore my creativity. As the only other female in our home of 5, I gravitated to her from the time I was very young. We would spend hours together singing, dancing, and playing "make believe". With each activity she reinforced to me that being a woman is a gift and convinced me that confidence in myself was quintessential to my ultimate happiness. As I grew into a woman, dealing with adolescent self-doubt and uncertainty, I found comfort in the memory of my mothers' words and even more so in her actions. Now, as an adult, being able to share my greatest passion with my favorite person is a reward sweeter than any I could have imagined.

By starting TL Yarn Crafts in 2013, I truly believe I have found the purpose of my skills for this season in my life. I am constantly looking for ways to push myself and am so inspired by the handmade community I have come to know. Though there will never be enough hours in the day to achieve everything I would like, I am still so in love with this crazy maker life.

We Are Knitters

By Alberto Bravo Reyes
We Are Knitters

Knitting-knitters-crochet-wool-kit. If you were to ask me, these would be the five words I use most in a day.

My name is Alberto, and I am the co-founder and creative director of We Are Knitters, or as you many of you know us as - WAK. Like many makers, I would say that I didn't choose knitting, but instead, that knitting chose me. I remember the first time I saw a group of knitters in New York – laughing and knitting together, as if it were the most natural thing in the world. I could not help but to find myself thinking, "something is happening here", which gave me the inspiration to pick up my first set of needles. Together, with my business partner Pepita, we found some wool, patterns, needles, and with the help of YouTube, we learned to knit. And in that moment, we asked ourselves, "if we can learn to knit, without knowing a stitch, and enjoy it, why could others not do the same?" And so, the idea for We Are Knitters was born.

One thing that I will never forget is the reactions from people when we started the business. The question that I received the most in the beginning was "what will you do when the trend is over"? But we knew from the start that once people started knitting, they would not be able to stop. The last year in particular has been amazing, with the knitting community growing and becoming more connected every day in a way that even we could not have predicted – and we are so happy to be a part of it.

When we started We Are Knitters, we only had 6 different kits. And we sold them mostly to our families and friends. One of my proudest moments was when we had our first sale to someone who we did not already know – it was like we had finally become a "real" business.

Of these 6 kits we started with, five of them are still available today and continue to be among our strongest sellers. This reminds us to always be growing and adapting, but never forgetting your beginnings.

To take an activity like knitting, with an image that is so unique and ingrained, and to make it into something that a wider audience can appreciate and enjoy has been an incredible experience. As makers, we are used to having a different perspective from most, but to me, that is one of the best parts of what makes us who we are. This distinct way of seeing the world when combined with being "technology natives" means that we have the chance to do more than support the maker movement, we have the chance to let it thrive in a way that might not have been possible before.

If making is your passion, it will always find a way to be in your life. As the sign in our office says "sin knitters, no somos nada", or "without knitters, we are nothing", we are confident that you, as makers, will always find your inspiration in the world around you. And on behalf of the entire team at We Are Knitters, we can't wait to accompany you on your journey for many years to come.

Finding the Path to Slow

By Nicole Knutsen
Naturally Nora Crochet

I made my life plans in second grade. Being a fantastic pragmatist at eight years old, I stated it as truth: "I will be a teacher." I recall that later, as we planned for college, many of my friends developed dreams centered around family life. Being a wife, being a mother - those things were not promised to me. Who can make plans on things un-promised? Teaching was a safe bet, as well as a vocation I felt deeply about, even at eight and 18.

In a blessing of my youth I could never have anticipated, a wife I indeed became, then a mother a few short years later. My reasonable, responsible life plan did not feel the same as it had once felt. The intensity with which I desired to just be with my firstborn child filled me like warm air rising in a tear drop shaped balloon, oxygen to flow through my veins and give me breath and movement and height. It shocked me, the suffocation of unfulfilled maternal purpose.

I pressed on, gasping for air each afternoon as I drove my 15 minutes home, arriving and drawing in deep, satisfying breaths of my child's infancy, buried deep in the loose, fine, golden ringlets at her nape. I rested, I woke, I did it again. I sacrificed and suffered, and, in some ways, I succeeded. But I was suffocating.

I was no longer eight, or even 18, drawing purpose from my students, my job, my reputation as the teacher in sensible shoes, making the sensible choice. I've known many women who balance this, a fulfilling career outside the home with motherhood. They do it well, not with ease, certainly, but remarkably well. I couldn't. I longed in the truest, locked up room of my heart to build for my family a simple life, slow in pace and minimal by nature, with more time outdoors than in, and more time with a steady, serene mama than the harried woman reading a quick bedtime story in the evenings. I prayed to my Father, know the desires of my heart; you put them there...take me to them!

The summer during which I was uncomfortably pregnant with my second daughter, I bought a pair of crocheted booties for her. They were a good price, chocolate brown acrylic, with a tiny bow at the toe. To go with them, I sewed a little bodysuit dress with remnant brown corduroy and thrifted sunflower buttons. It occurred to me that, in addition to rudimentary sewing skills, I indeed knew how to crochet. My grandmother had taught me the very basics, and a friend I met at 19 had built on that knowledge, leading to a rash of too-tight, super saver Christmas beanies my sophomore year of college. I could probably figure out how to make these tiny booties.

I dug out of some

cabinet the aluminum hand-me-down hooks that had belonged to my grandmother, The Queen of the Chevron Afghan. To my surprise, I also had a set of steel thread hooks that were my great-grandmother's. I recall vividly how her hands looked while working, too dainty for her rather large personality, spinning a mysteriously beautiful web of cotton thread.

Truthfully, despite the legacy of my immediate female ancestors, I had no idea how to begin making booties. I, however, am not one to question my ability to learn something new; I just do it, whatever it is.

A web search later, I was staring, baffled and fascinated, at my first crochet pattern, the path to the most rewarding and revolutionary rabbit hole of my life.

There is a fragment of Creator in each of us. I had always enjoyed experimenting with various creative hobbies: watercolors, poetry, simple sewing, even paper making in my parent's kitchen sink. Nothing had ever rooted me to the Creator within so deeply. Pragmatic to the core, it appealed to me greatly that my creativity resulted in something soft and cozy and useful.

In a matter of weeks, I was hooking up projects I would never have dreamed I would make-hats, scarves, skirts, and, yes, booties. I embraced an affinity for natural fibers; cotton and wool never seemed so elegant. My little girls had my mama mind swimming with my own original design ideas. Within months after giving birth to my second daughter, I also introduced the world to my patterns through Naturally Nora Crochet, almost on a whim.

I was utterly shocked when my first patterns actually began to sell. I had a ludicrous amount of learning to do, but I could feel the potential sprouting in me - this could be the gate to the winding, grassy path my husband and I want to lead our family down. I knew, now with sure clarity, exactly what I should be praying for. Use this creative affinity, this piece of You in me, to lead my family into the slow simplicity we so desire.

These were not life changes that happened overnight, nor even over the course of months; it has taken years for me to build a collection of designs about which I feel overwhelmingly proud, and the technical skill necessary to communicate these designs to other crochet artisans.

The truth is, I don't believe it is a job that will ever be complete. My creativity, still rooted deeply in my Creator, has many seasons of bloom left. My hope is that the slow simplicity this creative journey has provided for me and my family can be echoed when folks pick up one of my patterns - a time set aside to work those methodical stitches, woven with hopes and prayers and love for whomever might be the recipient of this precious handmade heirloom.

For DeBrosse

By Teresa Carter
DeBrosseNYC

The earthquake put Haiti on the map for many people, myself included. It feels so odd to think back to my very first trip, because I really knew nothing about the country or its people, I just remember feeling for them so deeply. I had no idea this would be the first of seven trips and counting, or that the poorest country in the western hemisphere would forever change the way I viewed the world.

And so my knitting journey started where you might least expect it. I entered a dilapidated, post earthquake shelter in Haiti, brimming with 67 joyful, orphaned children. We shared laughs, tickles, snuggles and lollipops. We greeted each other each day with the kind of running hug you see only in the movies, and those hugs nudged their way deep into my soul.

Leaving the children two weeks later was a heartache that I had never known. I wasn't myself for weeks, plagued with an overwhelming weight and desire to continue loving them in some tangible way. I began thinking back to what it was like to be their age, and remembered the blankets mom had made me to keep the monsters away. Who would make theirs?

So I asked my mom to teach me to crochet, and over the next nine months we taught anyone willing to learn. In the end, we had made over 150 blankets. With suitcases three times my weight, a few dozen creole phrases memorized, and the usual travel-day top knot, I showed up to that same dilapidated shelter where I left my heart a year earlier.

Some of our blankets magically transformed into superhero capes, some into forts, and a couple were seen flying through the halls. Regardless, all brought a sliver of hope into an otherwise hopeless place.

Day two of my 30 day adventure, I locked eyes with a little boy entertaining himself by balancing on top of a sack of potatoes.

Between cultural differences, language barriers, and age gaps, making a friend at a Haitian orphanage looks a lot different (sometimes it looks like trying to find your own balance on some potatoes). We just got each other. We had a bond. I can't really explain it. He was full of such joy and energy. Energy that teetered on the rascally side to be honest, but beyond endearing. His name was DeBrosse.

I quickly learned that his needs were much greater than blankets, but the blanket project proved that people were interested. Interested in these children's stories, interested in helping, and interested in being part of what we were doing. So I took this love for both the children and crocheting, and opened an Etsy shop in their name. The plan was simple – sell to the general public, and invite them to support DeBrosse and his friends. Our latest shipment, fully funded by customer purchases, included 50 bottles of medicine, 536 ounces of infant formula, 778 ounces of soap, and 3,678 diapers. More than just supplies, our hope is that the brand puts orphan care on the hearts of those we meet.

After this last delivery, my husband and I were drawn to the idea of investing in the parents as a more proactive approach to orphan care. With a bit of nervous idealism, we asked, "What if we taught

"We just got each other. We had a bond. I can't really explain it. He was full of such joy and energy. Energy that teetered on the rascally side to be honest, but beyond endearing.

His name was DeBrosse."

the mamas how to crochet, and offered them a spot on the team?" Because it isn't a lack of love that is ripping these families apart, it's poverty.

Orphan care is a much bigger issue than I can wrap my mind around still. I selfishly just want to adopt as many children as I can, and make sure that every forehead is kissed before bed. But the reality is that these children often have families who would love the opportunity to do just that.

In Haitian culture, parents often give their children over to an orphanage in hopes that they will be fed, educated, and given opportunity that they themselves cannot provide. It's a decision made out of love, and a decision that most of the world is not asked to make.

And so we pursued these brave mamas, packed our bags, and led a crochet training workshop right at the orphanage where their children live. We provided all the materials, a nourishing meal, a space for them to explore, and the opportunity to find the fulfillment that handmade brings to its makers.

Today, with great joy, DeBrosse now also provides a job, stability, and dignity to Kathia DeBrosse – a woman who has been wildly underestimated for far too long, and the very mother of little DeBrosse.

PHOTO BY CHAR CO

Happiness & Art

PHOTO BY GRETCHEN POWERS

PHOTO BY MATT WOOD PHOTO

By Sharrel Paul
Mud & Yarn

Life in my 20s was unexpected. I never expected to leave my hometown in Massachusetts for a life in California. I never expected to actually make it work in California. I never expected to be partying on Hollywood Boulevard or cruising around San Francisco. I never thought I would discover massage therapy as a career even after the four years it took to get that Bachelor's Degree. I also never expected to get a cancer diagnosis at 29. Life really has a way of throwing curve balls right when you think you have it figured out.

My 30s brought numerous invasive surgeries, being forced to give up massage therapy, an about face back to Massachusetts, and being faced with my mortality — all within a 6-month period. Phew! I had no idea what to do with myself or where to go. All I knew was that I needed to focus on healing myself. Trips into Boston for consultations, more surgeries and new treatments quickly became routine.

One of the only things that grounded me during all the chaos was crochet. The skill that my grandmother taught me way back when I was 10 was just about the only thing I could do to be productive. So while recovering from surgeries on my couch, I would marathon TV shows on Netflix and crochet gifts for all my friends and family. It also kept my mind off of the unpleasant questions that would creep to the forefront: Will I survive this? What happens if I don't? What if I do? How will my life change? Will I ever be able to support myself again?

Once all the surgeries had paused for a while and I was on bi-weekly immunotherapy treatments, I just couldn't stay cooped up any longer. I thought that maybe I would look into taking an art class as a form of therapy. Being a 30-something with cancer and unable to support myself was taking its toll. I desperately needed to start fresh with something I had never explored before.

Enter clay, stage right.

Taking a beginner wheel throwing class at a local pottery studio was so exciting! Well… I did have to drive almost an hour and a half in Boston morning traffic to get to the studio. I would have been on time, but I realized I had to park 10 blocks away just to park legally. I realized quickly that I was only one of two actual beginners in the class (among 10 or so people who had been doing it for at least a year already). And throwing pots isn't as easy as all those videos and movies make it look! By the end of my first class, I was having a mini melt down while walking back to my car. Why had I chosen this medium as art therapy?!? After a good ugly cry in my car, I decided since I already paid money I didn't have for the class that I would see it through for the duration. Also, I'm not usually a quitter.

I continued to crochet all the time: during my infusions at the hospital that lasted almost an entire day, and at home while trying to de-

20

compress. In the fall, I posted about my scarves on Facebook and all of a sudden I had a list of people willing to pay me for them! It lifted my spirits that friends and family were willing to support me while I was going through such an ordeal. Once I started posting photos of my wonky little clay creations, people expressed interest in pots, too! New, and more exciting, questions started to take over… People actually want to pay me for this? Could I actually make this into something that's profitable? Could I really end up doing something I love every day?

I started to gain inspiration through creating an Instagram account specifically for my creations and seeing other makers who were doing the same. A few makers that I followed had upwards of 20,000 followers and were selling out of their product within minutes of having a shop update. I knew I could combine my love for crochet and clay into something profitable. And so Mud & Yarn was born!

I just leaped! I did it! I found a ceramics studio that rented out space to artists and spent every hour I could in there covered in clay improving my technique. I also spent time apprenticing with my beginner wheel throwing instructor in her studio learning hand building techniques and seeing what it really took to say you're a full time potter. And with winters lasting so long in New England, there was no shortage of crochet orders, so my nights were spent catching up on those. My first holiday season in business, I made easily 75+ cowls. Now I was the one needing a massage therapist!

Before I knew it, my Instagram following was growing and the months of treatment were going by much faster. After months of bad news of tumors growing, crazy side effects, CT scans, needle pokes and anxiety, I finally got some GREAT news: the tumors were gone. I was officially NED – No Evidence of Disease! The experimental treatment that I was on worked! Being able to tell my family and friends the news was indescribable.

A lot of people say that prayer gets them through illness. For others it's a dramatic juice cleanse or change in diet. For me, it was the creative process. Being able to focus my energy into an art form that made me happy was the best healing therapy ever. I mean, I obviously have to give credit to my amazing team of doctors and nurses… and of course, the genius scientists that developed the breakthrough immunotherapy that shrunk all those stupid tumors.

But Happiness and Art. Those two deserve some major props.

Staying Present

By Talin Avakian
The Half Full Mug | Addy's Cozy Cowls

Using my imagination has always been a priority of mine. As a child, wherever I'd go, whether in class, sitting in church next to a relative, or standing at the barre in ballet class, I'd use my imagination to take me to other places. Making believe was my thing; I always looked for ways to make my current situation more fun or more interesting, which is why I loved watching shows and movies so much. The phrases, "what if," or "imagine this or that," were - and still are - frequents in my daily speech.

When not verbally expressing my imagination, I would create; in fact, sometimes I was better at drawing from my imagination in art form. As an early maker, I illustrated, most often doodling in my notebook or taking my writing assignments in elementary school way too seriously. The assignment would be to write a two to three paged fictional story, and I'd come in the next week with a twelve paged story with colored illustrations. While I was somewhat of an overachiever, I was more motivated to take things to the next level because I knew I was in a safe place; I was encouraged to leverage my creativity and I knew from an early age that it was the most impactful way to use my voice.

Many illustrated short story assignments and hundreds of handmade birthday cards later, I found myself picking up a new friend that would help me with my imaginative storytelling: the camera. The camera was an interesting tool for me to pick up because it not only allowed me to capture reality, it also gave me the opportunity to manipulate it, and eventually, start composing my own.

I liked having what felt like an extension of my eyes; I quickly became the "unofficial photographer" at many events I attended, which served as good practice. I enjoyed it most though when I'd go outside with my cousins or friends for photo shoots. Whenever we had spare time, that's what I'd do. "Wanna have a photoshoot?" we'd say when we were bored, and from there, we'd imagine concepts and head outside, shooting for hours.

After doing this so many times, I decided that I wanted to shoot pictures for a living. When it came to deciding what direction to head in for college, nothing made more sense to me than to go to art school, so that's what I did. I worked tirelessly on my portfolio my senior year, and thankfully got into my dream school (Massachusetts College of Art & Design), where I knew I'd be able to bring my dream of becoming a visual artist to life.

When I got to art school, I made every mistake I could make in the book. While I knew it was the right place for me to be and I loved every minute of being there, it also proved to be extremely humbling and challenging. Developing blank rolls of film (multiple times), misunderstanding assignments, exporting videos in the wrong settings, not being playful or bold enough with my work, and committing to way too much were a few examples of ways I messed up; I crashed quickly, and knew something had to change before I lost my mind and motivation.

One day, after a typical too full and exhausting day of school and campus activities, I came back to my dorm to find a friend crocheting on the couch. It immediately caught my attention because it seemed so relaxing, while still keeping busy...and best yet, she was actually creating a something to eventually wear! I remembered that my grandmother used to knit; this was expected though, that's what grandmothers did, right? Thinking back now, I definitely took the sweaters, socks, hats and other knitwear she made for my sisters and I for granted. Knowing now the amount of time, skill and dedication it takes to knit a garment, I'm able to appreciate what my grandmother did so much more. For some reason, seeing someone my age doing the same activity shined a new light on it; why hadn't I tried this before?

I was crafty, I loved seeing the fruits of my labor, and better yet, I loved the idea of being able to wear something and tell its story after creating it.

My curiosity didn't last too long before I booked it to the store to buy my first skeins of yarn and crochet hooks. A switch went off in me, and in fact, after meeting other crocheters on campus, I felt as if I was part of a movement. A movement to slow down? A movement to relax after a long stressful day of class? A movement to become a grandma at age 20? Whatever it was, I liked it, because it felt good, and it gave me not only a new sense of purpose, and frankly, a new hobby, but a new way to de-stress.

After many dropped stitches, dollars spent on yarn, and cowls gifted, I decided that I wanted to take things to another level. I opened my Etsy Shop (Addy's Cozy Cowls) in 2013 and embarked on the handmade seller journey, while promoting my cozy lifestyle. It was fun! I crocheted any free moment I had, many times during class or meetings. This was also another excuse to do more photoshoots with friends, which of course I loved. When the holidays hit, people started hitting me up for handmade gifts like crazy. Michaels and the post office became my second home. There were new creative challenges I faced every week, which was both thrilling and stressful.

I became even more interested in branding and marketing my knitwear, which definitely paid off. The more time and effort I spent on styling and shooting my cowls, the more people were inspired to order and make them part of their wardrobe. Time passed and more cowls got shipped, and while I still enjoyed my maker life, I still wanted to do more. I didn't want more work to do, but I had more inside of me that I wanted to share.

The fact of the matter was, I had more fun shooting with my knitwear than the actual process of making it and shipping it out. While I still enjoyed every aspect of my business while doing it, I found I was most motivated to do the part of the process after the piece was made: creating and telling the story of the piece. For me, it was more about the lifestyle I had created. But how would I talk about that with an Etsy shop being my only platform?

After lots of brainstorming, I decided it was time to launch a blog. A blog with what theme, though? My interests were all over the place. A filmmaker that crochets and knits in her spare time but also loves to dance, and oh yeah, loves fashion too? I had no idea how to tie it all together, but eventually I realized that my life did in fact have "a theme," among all of my scattered interests.

I've always valued living in the present and learning how to savor moments, among all the chaos. While it's no secret that I can't sit still or that I may commit to too much, I do recognize the importance of slowing down and smelling the roses, and for me that translates into a cozy lifestyle, and knowing how to have fun in both work settings as well as in free time.

And so "The Half Full Mug" was born - a lifestyle blog centered around the idea of living a cozy life, seeing things as half full, and learning how to savor moments.

Maker Life is the Best Life

By Jessica Carey
The Hook Nook

I have been crocheting since the fall of 2011 when my oldest was just a baby. At the time, my husband was working in a town about 20 minutes away and since we only had one car, I was home a lot with the baby. I did not have friends where we lived and needed to find an outlet to be "Jessica" instead of strictly "Mom" and "Wife".

I first tried to teach myself to knit and let's just say that was definitely not a success. But through YouTube videos I taught myself to crochet, and once I quickly figured it out, I couldn't stop!

Soon after I felt more comfortable with my products, I began posting them on Facebook to share with friends and family and soon started receiving orders. At this time, I was very excited to earn a little bit of cash to pay for the yarn I was using. It was such an amazing feeling to pay for my own yarn!

Fast forward a few months and I decided to open an Etsy shop to create more of a professional platform. Even though it was very slow going in the beginning, it made me feel so proud to have my own little business that was for "Jessica".

I specialized in newborn photography props, camera buddies, and other small items that were quick to work up since having a baby didn't offer a lot of extra time to create larger items. I also noticed that the larger items didn't keep my attention nor kept me motivated. This is why I always encourage people

to make what their hearts enjoy making. Our shops may be a business, but it is our desire and creativity that really makes this craft special. Don't lose sight of that!

In September of 2013, I opened my Instagram account to hop on this social media bandwagon. It was so fun to have a way to connect more personally to my customers and audience by posting more than just product photos. I was able to also create relationships with other shops, pages and people which has been invaluable in the success I've been fortunate enough to find.

In my earlier days, I collaborated a lot with Crunchy Mamas, a handmade organic beauty and wellness business. Ashley and Katie were phenomenal in my early successes and I value their opinion on business ethics, networking, finance and all other aspects of small business to this day. At the time, they would send me product samples to throw into my orders which was a great benefit to them and myself. I was able to offer them free advertisement while also providing unexpected free gifts to my customers. They would also donate fantastic prizes to any giveaway I hosted without question. They would give me shout-outs and sup-

port in every way they could. They even allowed me to be a speaker at their first The Project event which is an amazing event geared towards women who own small businesses. Being able to work with them in my early days is absolutely and immensely connected with the success I've found today. I will always be grateful to them and their friendship.

Today, I have really found a love for original and trendy womenswear that is both edgy and feminine. It has been my main goal and drive to inspire others as well as bringing the crochet craft out of the "grandma" stereotype and into the modern and trendy designs.

I want to create items that I would actually wear and being able to wear sweaters, beanies and cowls around town where people ask "Where did you buy that?!" and being able to tell them that I made it

is exciting!

In my opinion, slow sustainable fashion needs to find a way back into the mainstream. To be able to wear our handmade items is such a proud and amazing feeling - a feeling that creates confidence and worth. I'm sure all makers can relate!

It has been an amazing opportunity for our family, my husband (who is a phenomenal tattoo artist) and I to be creatives and artists, and to have both found success in our crafts.

For us, it is amazing to be able to show our children that they, too, can find that passionate career. They can truly create their own future in whatever way makes them the most happy. It's been difficult at times to continue my business knowing that it has affected different aspects of my life, but I am hoping that these choices can really offer our children confidence in being them-

selves and making choices that truly fill their soul and inspire them to be the best versions of themselves.

Being a maker is more than just creating. Being a maker is a lifestyle and comes with a responsibility to be original, to be motivated and to be inspiring. I am so blessed and grateful to have found my

love for crochet and am even more honored that so many others have enjoyed my work. It is an incredible feeling to do what I love and have others receive it so positively.

My life is a an actual dream come true, and there is no doubt about it, the maker life is the best life.

LOOKBOOK

CHAIN TWENTY

"Chain Twenty's main goal is to bridge the gap between traditional techniques such as knitting and crochet, and modern fashion and interior design. It combines an inspirational blog with a shop that will be filled with handmade oversized jumpers, chunky fashion accessories, and minimalistic home deco."

MEREL KOSTERS
CHAINTWENTY.COM

JOYFUL FOUR

"I'm a lifestyle photographer based in Bergen County, New Jersey. When I'm not running after my four kids or photographing clients, you'll find me crocheting and documenting it on Instagram."

CHARISSA FISCHKELTA
JOYFULFOUR.ETSY.COM

MILK WORKSHOP

"Knitting is my first love and I would do it all the time if I could. I learned when I was very small and haven't stopped! I love working with natural fibres and I have a dream to raise some alpaca and sheep one day, so that I can play with all the wool that I like!"

CATHRYN BROWN
MILKWORKSHOP.COM

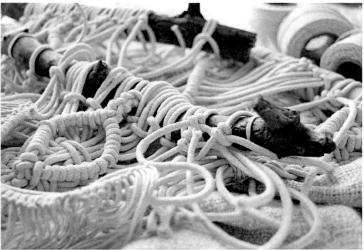

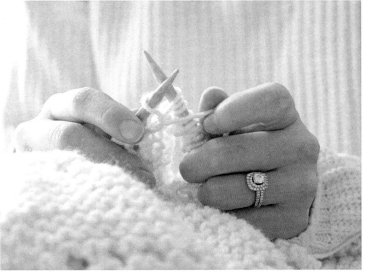

KNITTING WONDERS

"My interest in fiber arts began decades ago and has expanded to knitting, crocheting, weaving, and macramé. I am thrilled and honored to bring my passion to life by creating cozy, hand-knitted items and macramé wall hangings each day!"

SIERRA RICHARDSON
KNITTINGWONDERS.ORG

TOPKNOT STYLE

"My crocheted blankets from my Mom, Grandma and Aunt are piled into my linen closet always within reach for my children. Pilled, worn and stretched out. My hope for every blanket I crochet is they will one day be worn with love and always draped over the sofa to be pulled down for special movie nights, to help sniffles go away and for when we need to be wrapped up in a hug."

AMANDA ROBINSON
TOPKNOTSTYLE.CA

LA RESERVE DESIGN

"My grandmother gave me a handmade blanket when I was born that followed me throughout most of my childhood, becoming a reminder of home in my college bedroom. I love making blankets because I can imagine them being used again and again by their owners, moving with them through different stages in their lives."

ALISON ABBEY
LARESERVEDESIGN.COM

KNITATUDE

"Fall is the perfect reminder that my favourite season is coming. The air gets that slight chill and the leaves start to change.
It's like a fond message from an old friend.
Hello chunky knits and sweater weather!"

CHANTAL MIYAGISHIMA
KNITATUDE.CA

LEIGHSIDE KNITS

"Nature-loving, word-eating wife,
mother and knitter.
Currently chronicling my life in wool
(and a few other things besides)."

LEIGH MILLER
INSTAGRAM.COM/ LEIGHSIDEKNITS

NORTHKNITS

"I'm just a girl who found grace through knitting and have found a calling like no other through leadership and dedication in the knitting and crochet community."

JEWELL WASHINGTON
NORTHKNITSBYJEWELL.COM

KNITBROOKS

"I find serenity in the stillness of the outdoors, and feel fortunate to have had the opportunity to draw inspiration from so much of Canada's untouched wilderness through my travels across this beautiful country I call home."

KELLY BROOKS
KNITBROOKS.CA

PATTERNS

Fingerless Gloves

A Crochet Pattern by Marialena of Malloo

WHAT YOU NEED

Bulky yarn,US Size N/15 (10.0mm) crochet hook, yarn needle, scissors.
Yardage: less than 96m (105yds)
Gauge: 9 stand 7 rows is 4 inches in hdc

NOTES

1. Read the pattern carefully before you begin crocheting.
2. The pattern is worked in joined rounds, except if stated otherwise.
3. The first stitch of every round is worked in the same stitch as the slip stitch.

ABBREVIATIONS

R = round
ch = chain
slst = slip stitch
sc = single crochet
hdc = half double crochet
dc = doublecrochet
Fhdc = foundation half double crochet
st = stitch
tlo = third loop only

FROM THE DESIGNER

"I love to play with different techniques and materials to create texture and always tries to recreate some of her favorite knit stitches with a crochet hook!"
- Marialena (Lou) of Malloo.

FINGERLESS GLOVES

R1: Fhdc 16, slst to join, ch1 (16)
R2-4: hdc in tlo in each st around, slst, ch1 (16)
R5: in tlo*sc in first st, dc in next st*, repeat from * to * around, slst, ch1 (16)
R6: *dc in first st, sc in next st *, repeat from * to * around, sl st, ch1 (16)
R7: *sc in first st, dc in next st*, repeat from * to *around, sl st, ch1 (16)
R8: *dc in first st, sc in next st*, repeat from *to *across, ch1, turn (16)
R9: repeat row 8
R10: *dc in first st, sc in next st*, repeat from * to *around, sl st, ch1 (16)

R11: *sc in first st, dc in next st*, repeat from * to* around, slst, ch1 (16)
R12: hdc in each st around, slst, ch1 (16)
R13: hdc in tlo in each st around, slst, ch1(16)
R14: sc in tlo in each st around, slst. FO

Now, make a second one exactly the same! Fasten off and weave in all ends. That's it! Enjoy!
Optional: Sew buttons under the thumb for decorative purposes.

Luxury Baby Blanket

A Knitting Pattern by Sarah of Mama Knows Luxury

WHAT YOU NEED

6 x 100 Gram Balls Sugarbush Chill Yarn (312 Yards) (Super Bulky 6)
25 MM (US Size 50) Circular Knitting Needles, and Weaving Needle
Basic Felting Kit (optional for joining and finishing ends

LUXURY BABY BLANKET

This pattern is worked in rows, turning at the end of each row.
Holding 2 strands of yarn together, long tail cast on 36 stitches.

Rows 1-4: Knit (Garter Stitch)
Row 5: K4, Purl 28, K4
Row 6: Knit
Rows 7-36: Repeat rows 5 & 6
Row 37: Repeat Row 5
Rows 38-41: Knit

Bind off, and felt or weave in the ends. I joined using felting on rows 13 and 28.

FROM THE DESIGNER

"I believe creativity is a fundamental part of being human, and I rejoice in the opportunity to express my creative spirit."
- Sarah of Mama Knows Luxury

Autumn Ombre

A Knitting Pattern by Kathleen of Country Pine Designs

WHAT YOU NEED

US Size M/9mm double pointed needles, and/or 9mm 16" circular needles
Super bulky weight yarn.
Recommended: Wool-Ease Thick and Quick. Will need three colors for this hat. Color A (bottom color), B (middle color) & C (top color and pom pom)
Yarn needle to sew and weave in ends
Size: Adult
Gauge: 5 stitches = 2 inches

NOTES

1. When changing colors, keep an eye on your tension to avoid making your hat too snug.
2. There are three different colors used within this pattern, so pay attention to where colors are cut off, and added on.
3. Pom-pom is optional.
4. Recommended cast on method is long tail.

ABBREVIATIONS

K = knit
P = purl
K2tog = knit two together

FROM THE DESIGNER

"I know that God has many great things in store for me here in Texas, and I am thankful that he has blessed me with the ability to create in order to try to bless others along the way."
- Kathleen of Country Pine Designs

OMBRE HAT

With Color A Cast on 39. Join.
Row 1: Purl the whole row.
Rows 2-9: With color A, knit for the whole row.
Rows 10 & 11: Alternate knitting *color a k1, color b k1*. Repeat until you have
two whole rows of alternating color stitches. (Make sure that your
colors do not match up within the two rows. The colors need to be staggered in order to achieve the gradient look.)
CUT OFF COLOR A leaving a 6 inch tail, begin knitting with only color B.
Rows 12- 19: Knit the whole row

with color B.
Rows 20-21: Alternate knitting *color b k1, color c k1*. Repeat until you have
two whole rows of alternating color stitches. (Remember that the
colors should not match up within the two rows to achieve the gradient look.)
CUT OFF COLOR B leaving a 6 inch tail, you will now begin knitting with only
color C.
Rows 22-26: Knit the whole row with color C. Prepare to decrease.
Decreasing:
Row 27: *k3 k2tog* repeat until you have reached the end of the row.
By repeating through the end of this row, you will have to decrease the first stitch of the next row. (You should have 32 stitches on your needles now.)
Row 28: Knit the whole row, no decrease.
Row 29: *k2 k2tog* repeat until the end of the row. (You should have 24 stitches on your needles now)
Row 30: Cut the yarn leaving a 2 foot tail, pull tail through the remaining stitches, synch tight. Sew the top shut, so that there is no hole showing.

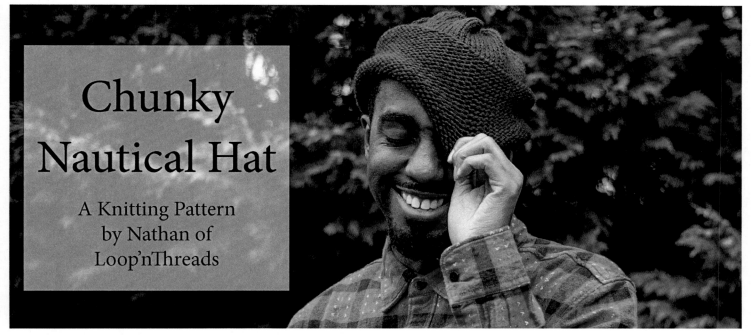

Chunky Nautical Hat

A Knitting Pattern
by Nathan of
Loop'nThreads

WHAT YOU NEED

Wool of the Andes Bulky Yarn 137 yards per skein (1)
U.S 10 | 16" Circular Needles,
Tape Measure, Yarn Needle, Scissors

ABBREVIATIONS

K = knit
P = purl

NOTES

Wearing a hat shows character.
The Chunky Nautical Hat is a step up in cozy land. It's even warmer and made of Peruvian Highland Wool. Very premium material that is soft and durable for a lifetime of wear. Its structure is unique as it is sturdy, yet it takes the shape of the wearer's head. The design is intended for both male and female, unisex.

Texture & design.
The simple purl and knit stitch design works seamlessly together. When they meet they create the illusion of a fold over brim. This item can be made with any bulky yarn of your choice of course. I recommend the yarn I use because things like fit, drape, texture, etc. will vary with other yarns. All of my patterns are based off the exact material I use to make it.

KNIT HAT

Cast-on 72
R1 - Join without twisting work and place the marker on. Optional: K1, P1 around for 2 rows to minimize curling. It will anyways, but these two rounds can help it over-curling, if it's not your preference.
R2 and On - After joining in a circle or K1, P1 rounds, continue to purl until work measures 4 ½ inches. Once work reaches 4 ½ inches, knit for another 4 ½ inches. This makes a total of 9 inches.
Decrease Rounds - *K8, K2 together (decrease). Repeat from * around so there are 6 total decreases. Stitches will get really tough, but it can totally be done without DPNs (double pointed needles).
Continuing Decrease Rounds
*K7, K2 together, Repeat from * around.
*K6, K2 together, Repeat from * around.
*K5, K2 together, Repeat from * around.
*K4, K2 together, Repeat from * around.
*K3, K2 together, Repeat from * around.
*K2, K2 together, Repeat from * around.

X - Cut the yarn leaving a lengthy tail. Thread yarn tail through a yarn needle and run through the remaining stitches together.
Weave in tail and any other ends.

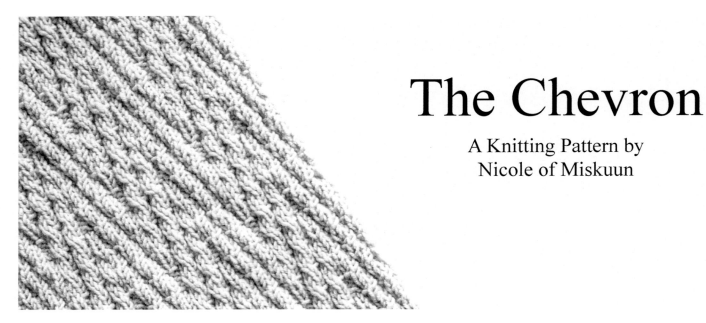

The Chevron

A Knitting Pattern by Nicole of Miskuun

WHAT YOU NEED

Needles: Size 4 US / 3.5mm
Stitch marker
Tapestry needle

Shown in: MillaMia Naturally Soft Merino, Putty
Yardage: Just over 9 skeins // 50g or 136 yards per skein
Weight : Sport

Measurements

Width : 10 inches / 25.4 cm
Length : 99 inches / 251.4 cm

ABBREVIATIONS

K: Knit
P: Purl
rep: Repeat
sts: Stitches

FROM THE DESIGNER

"I design knitting and crochet patterns with you, the maker, in mind. Inspired by clean lines and minimalism, I cut out all the excess to create simple, easy to follow designs for those tired of all the extras. A pattern should be stress-free to work up, and I aim to create patterns that are exactly that."
- Nicole of Miskunn

CHEVRON SCARF

Cast on 91 stitches
Row 1 (RS): P1, *(K2, P2) twice, K1, (P2, K2) twice, P1* ; rep from * to end
Row 2: K1, *(P2, K2) twice, P1, (K2, P2) twice, K1* ; rep from * to end
Row 3: As Row 1
Row 4: As Row 2
Row 5: (P2, K2) twice, *P3, K2, P2, K2* ; rep from * to last 2 sts, P2
Row 6: (K2, P2) twice, *K3, P2, K2, P2* ; rep from * to last 2 sts, K2
Row 7: As Row 5
Row 8: As Row 6
Row 9: As Row 2
Row 10: As Row 1
Row 11: As Row 2
Row 12: As Row 1
Row 13: As Row 6
Row 14: As Row 5
Row 15: As Row 6
Row 16: As row 5

Repeat these 16 rows until your scarf measures 99" / 251.4 cm
Bind off loosely according to pattern (knitting the knits and purling the purls). Weave in any remaining ends and enjoy!

Optional: Creating an Infinity Scarf

If you would like your scarf to be an infinity scarf, simply use some of the leftover yarn and a tapestry needle and seam the two ends together.

Pink Lemonade Tassel Scarf
A Crochet Pattern by Olivia of Hopeful Honey

WHAT YOU NEED

Yarn: Debbie Bliss Roma (70% Wool, 30% Alpaca; 87 yards/100g), Rose (3 – 4 skeins)
12.00mm (O/17) Crochet Hook
260 - 320yds Super Chunky Yarn (14ply)
Tapestry Needle
Gauge: 5 rows & 5 stitches in sc = 2 inches (5cm)

NOTES

Size: Changes for child and teen/adult size are in [ ].

2 - 5 Yrs (Toddler)
Width: 6.5" (16.5cm)
Length: 61" (155cm)
6 - 12 Yrs (Child)
Width: 7.5" (19cm)
Length: 65" (165cm)
Teen - Adult
Width: 8.5" (22cm)
Length: 69" (175cm)

ABBREVIATIONS

st(s) – stitch(es)
ch – chain stitch
sc – single crochet
2dccl – 2 double crochet cluster stitch

SPECIAL STITCHES

2 Double Crochet Cluster Stitch (2dccl)
Yarn over, insert your hook into the next stitch. Yarn over, and pull back through that stitch (3 loops on your hook). Yarn over, and pull through 2 loops (2 loops on your hook). Yarn over, and insert your hook into the same stitch. Yarn over, and pull back through that stitch (4 loops on hook). Yarn over, and pull through 2 loops (3 loops on hook). Yarn over, and pull through all 3 loops on your hook.

TASSEL SCARF

Ch13 [15, 17] using 12.00mm hook.
Row 1 – 1 sc in 2nd ch from hook. 1 sc in the next 11 [13, 15] sts. Turn your work. (12 [14, 16] sts)
Row 2 – Ch1, 1 sc in the same st. 1 sc in next 2 [3, 4] sts. Ch2, skip 3 sts. 1 2dccl, ch1, 1 2dccl, ch1, 1 2dccl in the next st. Skip 2 sts, 1 sc in the next 3 [4, 5] sts. Turn your work. (9 [11, 13] sts)
Row 3 – Ch1, 1 sc in the same st, 1 sc in the next 2 [3, 4] sts, turn your work. Ch1, 1 sc in the same st, 1 sc in the next 2 [3, 4] sts, turn your work. Ch1, 1 sc in the same st, 1 sc in the next 2 [3, 4] sts. Ch2, skip 2 '2dccl' made in the previous row. 1 2dccl, ch1, 1 2dccl, ch1, 1 2dccl in the next '2dccl' made in the previous row. Skip ch2 space, 1 sc in the next 3 [4, 5] sts. Turn your work.
Row 4 - 49 [53, 57] – Repeat row 3. Fasten off, and weave in loose ends.
Row 50 [54, 58] – Ch1, 1 sc in the same st, 1 sc in the next 2 [3, 4] sts, turn

your work. Ch1, 1 sc in the same st, 1 sc in the next 2 [3, 4] sts, turn your work. Ch1, 1 sc in the same st, 1 sc in the next 2 [3, 4] sts. 1 sc in top of '2dccl' from previous row, 1 sc in 'ch1' space, 1 sc in top of '2dccl' from previous row, 1 sc in 'ch1' space, 1 sc in top of '2dccl' from previous row, 2 sc in 'ch2' space. 1 sc in the next 3 [4, 5] sts.
Fasten off, weave in loose ends.

Tassels/Fringe:
Taking your yarn, cut 8 strands of yarn (14" long). Fold 6 of the strands in half/ double, and take the 7th strand and knot it around the centre of the fold. Taking the 8th strand of yarn, wrap it around the group of 6 (now doubled to 12) strands of yarn, and knot it tightly.
Trim each tassel to measure 5" (12.5cm).
Sew 5 tassels along each edge of the scarf (first row and last row of "Scarf").

The Coelum Sweater

A Crochet Pattern by Janne of Joy of Motion

WHAT YOU NEED

Drops Loves You #7 (2 Fine)
Sports/5 Ply/12 wpi
7-11 skeins
4.5 mm [7] crochet hook and a needle

Gauge:
Measured with Double Treble Crochet Stitch:
2.3 st x 1.3 rows per inch
0,9 st x 0,6 rows per cm

Measured with Mini Flower Stitch:
4.6 st x 2.5 rows per inch
1,8 st x 1,5 rows per cm

Measured on arms:
4.3 st x 6.9 rows per inch
1,7 st x 2,7 rows per cm

ABBREVIATIONS

ch – chains
DTCS – Double Treble Crochet Stitch
MFS – Mini Flower stitch
prev - previous

sc – single crochet
sl st – slip stitch
sk – skip
st - stich (es)
yo - yarn over

NOTES

You will need to use the "Double Treble Crochet Stitch" & the "Mini Flower Stitch", as well as single crochet stitches & slip stitches.

Double Treble Crochet Stitch:
Each row of "Double Treble Crochet Stitch" will start with ch 2.

Written description: 2x yo draw up a loop from next st, yo, pull through 2 loops, yo, pull through 2 loops, 2x yo draw up a loop from same st, yo, pull through 2 loops, yo, pull through 2 loops, yo, pull through 3 loops.

Mini Flower Stitch: Each row of "Mini Flower Stitch" will start with ch 1 & end with sc 1.

Written description: In next st, draw up a loop, yo, draw up a loop from same st, yo, pull yarn through 4 loops on the hook, ch 1, draw up a loop from same st, yo, draw up a loop from same st, yo, pull yarn through 4 loops on the hook, sk 1 st, sc in next st, sk 1 st.

Size and measurments:

XS (S) M (L) XL

	Armhole circumference	Waist/Bust/Hip circumference	Suggested length*	Shoulder
XS	32,5 cm/12.8 inches	77 cm/30.3 inches	60 cm/23.75 inches	10,5 cm/4.1 inches
S	35,5 cm/14 inches	86 cm/33.9 inches	60 cm/23.75 inches	11,5 cm/4.5 inches
M	38,5 cm/15.2 inches	95 cm/37.4 inches	60 cm/23.75 inches	12 cm/4.7 inches
L	41,5 cm/16.3 inches	104 cm/40.9 inches	60 cm/23.75 inches	13 cm/5.1 inches
XL	44,5 cm/17.5 inches	113 cm/44.5 inches	60 cm/23.75 inches	14 cm/5.5 inches

*The length can be adjusted by adding/reducing rows – see instructions.

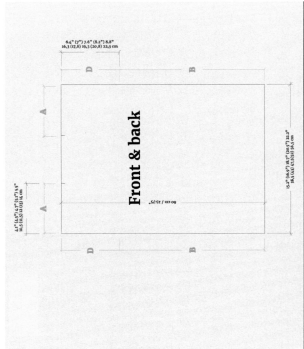

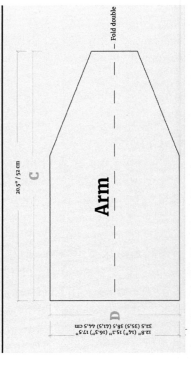

COELUM SWEATER

Front & back:
Crocheted from bottom to top. Make 2.

Ch 66 (74) 82 (90) 98 st.

Row 1: Sc in 3rd ch from hook (1st 2 ch counts as last ch from preparation row + 1st sc for row 1), 1 sc in each ch from preparation row, turn (= 65 (73) 81 (89) 97 st).

Row 2: Ch 2 (counts as 1st st), crochet modified DTCS 1 in each st from prev row, turn (= 32 (36) 40 (44) 48 DTCS), (= 33 (37) 41 (45) 49 st total).

Row 3: Ch 2 (counts as 1st st), DTCS 1 in each DTCS from prev row, turn (= 32 (36) 40 (44) 48 DTCS), (= 33 (37) 41 (45) 49 st total).

Row 4: Ch 1 (counts as 1st st), crochet amodified MFS in each the DTCS from prev row, turn (= 65 (73) 81 (89) 97 st).

Row 5-6: Ch 1 (counts as 1st st), crochet MFS in each st from prev row (no modification for these rows), turn (= 65 (73) 81 (89) 97 st).

Row 7: Ch 1 (counts as 1st st), crochet sc in each st from prev row, turn (= 65 (73) 81 (89) 97 st).

Row 8: Ch 1 (counts as 1st st), crochet sl st in each st from prev row, turn (= 65 (73) 81 (89) 97 st).

Row 9: Repeat row 7.

Row 10: Repeat row 8.

Row 11-13: Ch 1 (counts as 1st st), crochet MFS in each st from prev row, turn (= 65 (73) 81 (89) 97 st).

Row 14: Ch 2 (counts as 1st st), crochet modified DTCS st in each st from prev row, turn (= 32 (36) 40 (44) 48 DTCS), (= 33 (37) 41 (45) 49 st total).

Row 15: Ch 2 (counts as 1st st), crochet DTCS st in each st from prev row, turn (= 32 (36) 40 (44) 48 DTCS), (= 33 (37) 41 (45) 49 st total). Repeat row 4-15 5 times total = 71 rows/ approximately 60 cm or 23.75 inches. Fasten thread. You can change the length to fit your preference.

Arms:
Ch 27 (32) 37 (42) 47 st.

Row 1: Sc in 3rd ch from hook (1st 2 ch counts last last ch from preparation row + 1st sc for row 1). 1 sc in each ch from preparation row, turn (=26 (31) 36 (41) 46 st).

Row 2: Ch 1 (counts as 1st st), crochet sl st in each st from prev row, turn (=26 (31) 36 (41) 46 st).

Row 3: Ch 1 (counts as 1st st), crochet 2 sc in 1st st from prev row, then crochet 1 sc in each st from prev row, turn (=27 (32) 37 (42) 47 st).

Row 4: Repeat row 2. Same stitch count as prev row made.

Row 5: Ch 1 (counts as 1st st), crochet sc in each st from prev row, turn (=27 (32) 37 (42) 47 st).

Row 6: Ch 1 (counts as 1st st), crochet 2 sl st in 1st st from prev row, then crochet 1 sl st in each st from prev row, turn (=28 (33) 38 (43) 47 st).

Row 7: Repeat row 5. Same stitch count as prev row made.

Row 8: Repeat row 2. Same stitch count as prev row made.

Row 9-74: Repeat rows 3-8 until you have 56 (61) 66 (71) 76 stitches. Your arm should measure about 30 cm or 11.8 inches now.

Row 74-: Repeat rows 2 & 5 every other row until your arm measures 52 cm or 20.5 inches with stitch count (56 (61) 66 (71) 76 st. You can change the length to fit your preference. Fasten thread.

Arms:
Crochet together the sweater on the shoulder on both sides; front and back panel together with as many stitches as you prefer (A in diagram).

Crochet together the sweater on both sides (B in diagram), leaving the measurements for the armholes.

Fold the arms double & crochet them together (C in diagram). Then crochet the arms to the armholes (D in diagram). The crochet seam on the arms should face downwards. Fasten threads.

Mod Crochet Mocs

A Crochet Pattern by Jess of Make and Do Crew

WHAT YOU NEED

Lion Brand 24/7 Cotton – 1 skein (100g/186 yds)
Size B [2.5 mm] crochet hook or size needed to fit through flip flop hole
1 pair of flip flops
Sharp tool to poke holes in flip flops (skewer, thin drill bit or tapestry needle)
Approx 2 yards leather laces cut into 1-yard pieces
Size: Adult women's 5 and up (Pattern provides details to make any women's shoe size).
Gauge: 8 sts and 7 rows/rnds = 1 inch [2.5 cm] in single crochet
Gauge will vary a bit based on distance between poked holes on flip flop sole.

ABBREVIATIONS

sc – single crochet   **st** – st
sk – skip   **MC** – main color
sl st – slip stich   **cont** – continued

CROCHET MOCS

Moccasin Sides and Heel

Note: This section is worked in a spiral. There is no need to join or ch 1 at the beginning of each round.

To begin: Use sharp instrument to poke holes every ¼ inch (.25") around each flip flop sole. You want the hole to go at an angle from about the middle of the way down the sole to about a ¼ inches into the top of the sole. Make your holes far enough from the edge that the yarn won't rip through the rubber. (See Photo A below.)

A

With smaller hook, attach MC yarn at the back of the heel by inserting your hook from the top of the flip flop toward the bottom of the sole, grabbing the yarn and pulling through to the top of the sole. Ch 1 through the loop you've created. (See Photo B.) The resulting tail inside the flip flop marks first st of this and subsequent rows. Add a proper stitch marker here if desired.

Round 1: (using smaller hook) sc into each hole on the flip flop sole, sl st to join. Do not turn.

Rounds 2-3: (switch to larger hook) sc in each sc around. Do not turn.

Rounds 4: (See Photo C for rough placement of increases. Exact location not impt.) sc in each st until front toe area, sc 2 in one of the st near where your pinky toe will go, sc in each st, sc 2 in one of the st where your big toe will go, sc in each sc to back of heel. Do not turn.

Rounds 5-8: sc in each sc around. Do not turn.

Begin short rows for heel shaping:

Notes: Place a stitch marker on either side of the moccasin, 3/5th of the way back toward the heel. (See Photo C for placement.) The following rows are worked back and forth around back of heel. Pattern notes assume flip flop is positioned with the heel toward you and the toe away from you when the

"right" or "left" stitch marker is mentioned.

Row 9: (Without turning work) sc in each st until left marked st, sl st into marked st, turn.

Row 10: ch 1, sk first st, sl st into next st, sc in each st until right marked st, sl st into marked st, turn.

Row 11: (work toward left marker) ch 1, sk first st, sl st into next st, sc in each st until 1 sc of previous round remains, turn. (See Photo D.)

Row 12: (work toward right marker) ch 1, sk first st, sl st into next st, sc in each st until 1 sc of previous round remains, turn. (See Photo D.)

Begin rows for leather laces "tube":

Notes: Remove original markers for short rows. Place markers 1/3rd of the way back from the toe on either side of the moccasin. (See Photo C.) The following round is worked in the round as 1-8 were. Work sc stitches in an even density to create a smooth edge over the "bump" where the short rows taper. Round 13 is a total of approx 1.25 laps around the flip slop sole.

Round 13: (work toward left marker and cont counterclockwise) ch 1, sk first st, sl st into next st, sc in each st around entire moccasin, ending at original marked st at back of heel. Do not turn.

Notes: The following rows are worked back and forth. Pattern notes assume flip flop is positioned with the heel toward you and the toe away from you when the "right" or "left" stitch marker is mentioned.

Rows 14, 16, 18: (work counterclockwise) ch 1, sc in each st ending in left marked st, turn.

Row 15, 17, 19: ch 1, sc in each st ending in right marked st, turn.

Row 20: sc in each st ending at marked st at back of heel.
Fasten off yarn and

weave in ends.

Finishing leather laces "tube":
Fold the flap just created over and tuck one yard of the leather laces inside. With MC yarn and a tapestry needle, sew the laces into the tube using a whip stitch. (See Photo E or reference video for more detail.)

Moccasin Top
Row 1: (using larger hook) ch 19, turn.
Row 2: working into second ch from the hook, sc in each ch, turn.
Rows 3, 5, 7: ch 1, sk first sc, sc in next st, sc in each st until 1 st remains, sc 2 in last st, turn.
Row 4, 6, 8: ch 1, sc 2 in first st, sc in each st, turn.
Row 9: ch 1, sk first st, sc in next sc, sc in each st, turn.
Row 10: ch 1, sc in each st, turn.
Row 11: repeat row 9.
Row 12: repeat row 10.
Sizing Note: If your foot is on the wider side, add 2 or 4 rows of sc here to make the top toe section wider. (Simply repeat row 10 twice or four times.)
Row 13: ch 1, sc 2 in first sc, sc in each st, turn.
Rows 14, 16, 18, 20: ch 1, sk first sc, sc in next st, sc in each st until 1 st remains, sc 2 in last st, turn.
Rows 15, 17, 19: ch 1, sc in each st until 2 st remain, sk 1 st, sc in last st, turn.
Row 21: ch 1, sc in each st until 2 st remain, sk 1 st, sc in last st. Do not turn. Place marker in last st of this row.
Note: The follow round is worked around the entire top piece. Take care to keep stitches loose enough that the fabric doesn't pucker. See Diagram F visual explanation.
Round 22: (Without turning) work in sc around curved toe section and up the flat side of the piece. At the corner of the moccasin "point," sc 2 in the corner and sl st down the slant of the point and back up the other slant, sc 2 in the other "point," sc in each sc across the last flat side ending in st before marker. (See Diagram F.) Fasten off and weave in ends.

Finishing
Sewing Together:
Block the top piece if desired. Identify the best looking side of your top piece--specifically look at the points because one edge should be smoothest due to the slip stitching. This side should face your foot—the points will be folded over, revealing the smoothest edge.

Align the toe with the shoe rim and pin using stitch markers or safety pins. Using one strand of yarn (not doubled up), attach yarn inside the shoe at right corner side of the top piece. Whip stitch around toe, working from the top piece into the shoe rim as pictured. (See Photo G.) Work from the top down, going through the bottom loop of the top piece and the bottom loop of the shoe rim.) Before tying off yarn, do one stitch through the moccasin top into each folded over "point" to keep them tacked down. Fasten off yarn.

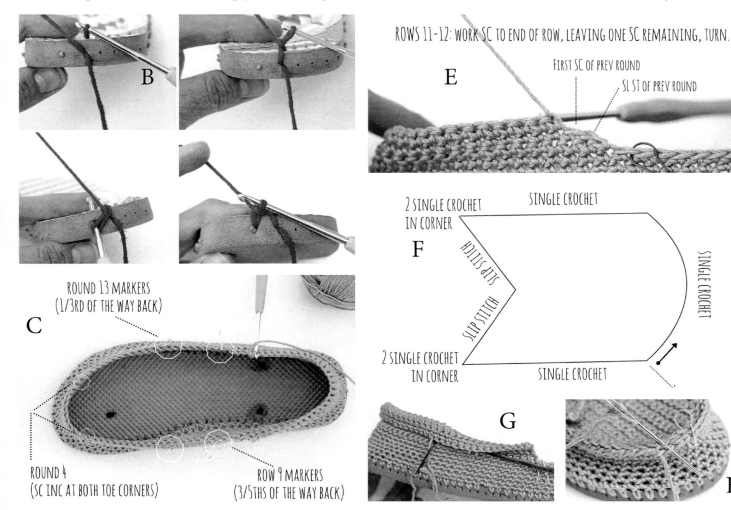

ROWS 11-12: WORK SC TO END OF ROW, LEAVING ONE SC REMAINING, TURN.

FIRST SC OF PREV ROUND
SL ST OF PREV ROUND

E

B

ROUND 13 MARKERS
(1/3RD OF THE WAY BACK)

C

ROUND 4
(SC INC AT BOTH TOE CORNERS)

ROW 9 MARKERS
(3/5THS OF THE WAY BACK)

2 SINGLE CROCHET
IN CORNER

SINGLE CROCHET

SLIP STITCH

F

SLIP STITCH

SINGLE CROCHET

2 SINGLE CROCHET
IN CORNER

SINGLE CROCHET

SINGLE CROCHET

G

H

MAKE
Volume One

Our Maker Life (OML) is a knit and crochet movement, for makers by makers, launched in May 2016. OML aims to bring together shop owners, knitwear designers, bloggers, and social media enthusiasts passionate about contributing to the creative, collective and beautiful handmade community. The OML team is made up of five makers and independent shop owners who came together and reached out to dozens of other creatives with an idea to meet and greet offline through maker meet up events. Since then, the OML movement has grown to nearly 40,000 strong online.

Read more about the OML team and mission at ourmakerlife.org.

Jewell Washington, OML Founder
Kelly Brooks, Alison Abbey, Kathleen Jones,
and Nathan Bryant, OML Organizers

COPYRIGHT

Made in the USA
San Bernardino, CA
29 July 2017